When I Became A Man

Men's Bible Study

James Daughtry

Abidan
Fox Lake, IL

To Kenneth G. Smith,
whose book, *Learning To Be A Man*,
helped me as a young man
and inspired me to write this book.

Contents

Introduction 7

Instructions 9

Chapter 1 God And Man 11

Chapter 2 The Perfect Man 19

Chapter 3 Man And Himself 27

Chapter 4 Man And Men 37

Chapter 5 Man And Women 47

Chapter 6 Man And Work 55

Chapter 7 Man And Wisdom 63

Chapter 8 Man And Muscles 75

Chapter 9 Man And Marriage 83

Chapter 10 Man And Spirituality 93

Bibliography 105

Notes 107

Introduction

A man is not a man simply because of his physical anatomy. A man does not become a man when he reaches a certain age, sleeps with a woman, serves in the military, graduates college, or gets married. A man becomes a man when he becomes what God intended him to be. [1]

God created man with a specific purpose and design. Therefore, men must follow the principles God has set forth in His word to truly fulfill the role of a man. This is not an easy task, however, because Satan continually tries to distort our understanding of what God intended for man.

In 1 Kings 2:2-3, the last words of King David to his son Solomon were that he must be strong, show himself to be a man, and follow the law of God. In these verses, King David gave Solomon instructions for fulfilling the role of a man. First, he emphasized that Solomon needed to be strong, referring to inner strength. Next, he stressed that Solomon needed to show himself to be a man, referring to his behavior. Finally, King David indicated that Solomon must follow the law of God, referring to his relationship with God.

The instructions that King David gave to Solomon are words that all men need to hear. Proverbs 20:6 states, "Most men will proclaim everyone his own goodness, but a faithful man who can find?"

A faithful man is truly hard to find, but God has given us His word that can transform us into the men He intended us to be. Therefore, let us diligently study the principles and role models God has provided in His word so that we will be able to show ourselves to be men.

Instructions

This Bible study guide may be used for personal study. However, a man will receive additional insights and gain a fuller understanding of the material by going through the study guide with another man or a group of men. The following format is recommended for a group.

1. Before the group meeting, each man should:
   - Read through the written section in the beginning of the chapter to get a good idea of the chapter's theme.
   - Look up the Bible verses and write his answers to the questions.

2. When the group meets, the men should:
   - Discuss the written section in the beginning of the chapter.
   - Take turns reading the questions and Bible verses out loud, and stating their answers.
   - Allow time for comments, questions, or a brief discussion.

3. When the group finishes a chapter, one or two men should attempt to give a brief summary of the chapter.

Chapter 1

God And Man

The starting place for understanding the purpose of man is in the Bible, beginning with the book of Genesis. In Genesis 1:26-28, we read that God created man in His own image and likeness. Man is unique by this fact. None of the animals were made in the image and likeness of God neither was anything else in creation. In addition, God gave man dominion and authority over "the fish of the sea, and over the fowl of the air, and over every living thing." Thus, God exalted man above all His creation.

After God creates Adam, we immediately see Adam reflecting his Creator. Just as God gave names to His creation, Adam begins to give names. Also, Adam reflects his Creator in doing work. As God did work in creating the world, Adam works in the Garden of Eden.

In the first three chapters of Genesis, we see that God places a high degree of responsibility on man. Although the challenges for man are great, God created man with extraordinary intellect and capabilities that would allow him to fulfill his role. Sadly, however, many men have a misunderstanding of their role. Other men simply neglect their God-given responsibilities. As a result, many men are not fulfilling their role as a man. The key element in being a man is to take up the responsibilities that God has set forth for him throughout the Bible.

Before answering the following questions, carefully read the first three chapters of Genesis. People often read quickly through the beginning of a book because they want to reach the plot. However, if the beginning is not fully understood, the reader will never completely comprehend and appreciate the book. Likewise, to understand what God intended for man, we must start by carefully examining the first three chapters of Genesis.

1. Based on Genesis 1:27, what attitude should a man have toward himself as well as other men and women?

_____

_____

_____

_____

2. Explain in your own words the meaning of each part of the command in Genesis 1:28.

_____

_____

_____

_____

_____

_____

3. In Genesis 2:5 and 2:15, what are the reasons God created man?

_____

_____

_____

4. In Genesis 2:18, why did God create woman?

_____

_____

_____

5. What names does God give in the following verses?

Genesis 1:5 _____

_____

Genesis 1:8 _____

_____

Genesis 1:10 _____

_____

Genesis 5:2 _____

_____

6. What names does the man give in the following verses?

Genesis 2:19 _____

_____

Genesis 2:23 _____

_____

Genesis 3:20 _____

_____

How are the man's actions similar to God's actions?

_____

_____

_____

_____

7. In Genesis 2:16-17, what specific instruction does God give directly to the man?

_____

_____

8. According to Genesis 3:17, how did the man fail to meet his responsibility?

_____

_____

9. List the consequences for men and women because of this act of disobedience in Genesis 3:16-19.

_____

_____

_____

_____

_____

Do these consequences exist today? Explain.

_____

_____

_____

_____

10. Do you see any differences between the biblical role of a man and society's view of a man? Explain.

_____

_____

_____

_____

_____

11. If a man is not fulfilling his role as a man, his behavior is contrary to God's plan. How have you fulfilled or not fulfilled the responsibilities God has given you as a man?

_____

_____

_____

_____

_____

_____

_____

_____

Chapter 2

The Perfect Man

Jesus Christ is the perfect example of a man and there is no better role model for us to follow than Him. Richard Halverson declared:

> This is a basic paradox in scripture, that the more like Jesus a man is, the more manly he will be, and the less like Jesus, the less of a man he is. The measure of manhood is the measure of a man's godliness. As God created man originally, only God can fashion manhood. [2]

Jesus lived on earth as a man with the desires, temptations, and struggles that men have, but He was perfect, sinless. Often, we have trouble seeing Jesus as a man because we think of Him only as God. As we read of

Jesus in the Bible, we need to see His humanity and how He lived as a man. By seeing Jesus as a man, we will better understand what God intended for man.

There are many events in the life of Jesus that display the masculine qualities we need to have as men. However, the ultimate demonstration of His manhood probably can be seen in the events shortly before and at His crucifixion. While Jesus was experiencing deep distress in the Garden of Gethsemane, His prayer showed His commitment to fulfilling the responsibility the Father had given Him. Later, despite lies, insults, beatings, and mockery, Jesus was able to maintain His composure. Finally, Jesus completed the work that He set out to do by going to Calvary and suffering a horrendous death on the cross. Through these events, Jesus displays for us qualities of determination, drive, self-control, courage, and wisdom, all of which we need to develop as men.

Nevertheless, despite these strong, manly qualities displayed by Jesus, He was also gentle. Jesus allowed people to bring little children to Him and He prayed for them. Jesus had mercy on people and comforted them with His words. He touched people and healed their illnesses. Jesus demonstrated tenderness, sensitivity, compassion, and sympathy, feelings that we as men often lack.

Jesus is vividly portrayed for us in the Bible so that we can be like Him. We need to study Him and the intricacies of how He behaved as a man. Jesus is the image that we should have in our minds when we think of what it means to be a real man.

The following Bible verses look at Jesus, the perfect man. As you read the verses and answer the questions, try to see Jesus the way that people in the Bible saw Him.

1. People in the Bible clearly saw Jesus as a man. Write down the people that said Jesus was a "man" in the verses below. (Check to see if the word "man" is used.)

Matthew 26:72-74 _____

Mark 15:39 _____

John 1:30 _____

John 4:28-29 _____

John 7:46 _____

John 8:39-40 _____

John 9:10-11 _____

John 10:31-33 _____

John 19:5 _____

1 Tim. 2:5 _____

Did these verses help you to see Jesus as a man from the perspective of people in the Bible? Explain.

_____

_____

_____

_____

_____

_____

_____

2. What are the things that Jesus did or felt in the following verses?

Matthew 4:2 _____

Matthew 8:10 _____

Matthew 8:24 _____

Matthew 17:17 _____

Matthew 26:38 _____

Mark 8:2 _____

John 4:6 _____

John 4:7 _____

John 11:35 _____

John 13:1 _____

Did these verses help you to see Jesus as a man? Explain.

_____

_____

_____

_____

_____

_____

3. How do the following verses show that Jesus was a man like us?

Romans 1:3 _____

_____

Colossians 2:9 _____

_____

4. Describe the life of Jesus based on Hebrews 5:7-9.

_____

_____

_____

_____

5. Based on Hebrews 4:15, why can Jesus understand our every struggle and why is Jesus the perfect role model for us to follow?

_____

_____

_____

_____

_____

_____

_____

6. Think about the life of Jesus. List some of the things that Jesus said or did that show us how a man should behave.

_____

_____

_____

_____

_____

_____

_____

_____

7. Based on the example of Jesus, explain some ways you have or have not shown yourself to be a man.

_____

_____

_____

_____

_____

_____

_____

_____

_____

_____

Chapter 3

Man And Himself

In 1 Corinthians 13:11, the Apostle Paul tells us that when he was a child, he behaved like a child. However, he goes on to say, "when I became a man, I put away childish things." The Apostle Paul indicates that as he developed into a man, he began to act like a man. His reference to "childish things" most likely does not refer to toys or laughter, but probably to things like selfishness and irresponsibility.

Overcoming childish behavior is an important step in becoming a man. Charles Spurgeon stated, "It is the highest stage of manhood to have no wish, no thought, no desire, but Christ." [3] As we become the men God intended us to be, our minds will focus less on ourselves and more on being like Christ.

Since God creates each man differently, no two men are exactly the same. Every man has his own strengths and weaknesses. Therefore, each man must evaluate himself to see the areas of his life that need improvement. For many of us, there may be some childish behavior in our lives that will be very difficult to change. Nevertheless, we must not get discouraged. Jesus lived on earth as a man and understands our every struggle. We need to look to Him not only as our example, but also as God Almighty who is able to transform our lives.

As we struggle and strive to be the men God intended us to be, we need to keep the proper view of ourselves. The everyday pressures of a man's life can often bring frustration and self-doubt. During these times, we must realize that we have been created in the image and likeness of God and we must stand tall as men. Jesus gives us the perfect example. Don Hillis states:

> Jesus humbled Himself, but He never humiliated Himself. He laid aside His glory, but not His self-respect. He was willing to be cursed, but never cursed Himself. He was despised and rejected by men, but He didn't despise or reject Himself. No word of self-condemnation ever escaped His lips. Jesus believed that man was God's highest creation and He exalted manhood. [4]

As men, we will face many challenges and temptations throughout our lives. Often, some of our greatest struggles will be a result of our own childish desires. The following verses look at a number of different men in the Bible and their manly behavior or their childish behavior, their strengths or their weaknesses.

In order to better understand yourself and how you can better fulfill your role as a man, carefully consider each Bible verse and answer the questions.

1. Describe the struggles or negative qualities that can be seen in the lives of the following men.

Nabal, 1 Samuel 25:2-3 _____

_____

_____

Solomon, 1 Kings 11:1-3 _____

_____

_____

Haman, Ester 3:5-6 _____

_____

Pharisees, Matthew 23:5-7 _____

_____

_____

Demas, 2 Timothy 4:10 _____

_____

Can you see any of these struggles or negative qualities in your own life? Explain.

_____

_____

_____

_____

_____

2. Name some other men in the Bible that have struggles or negative qualities.

_____

_____

_____

_____

_____

3. Describe the positive qualities that can be seen in the lives of the following men.

Joseph, Genesis 39:7-12 _____

_____

_____

_____

Centurion, Matthew 8:5-9 _____

_____

_____

Luke, Luke 1:1-4 _____

_____

_____

Steven, Acts 7:59-60 _____

_____

_____

Cornelius, Acts 10:1-2 and 10:22 _____

_____

_____

Apollos, Acts 18:24-28 _____

_____

_____

Publius, Acts 28:7 _____

_____

Can you see any of these positive qualities in your own life? Explain.

_____

_____

_____

_____

_____

4. Name some other men in the Bible that have positive qualities.

_____

_____

_____

_____

_____

5. Describe how the Apostle Paul felt in Romans 7:15 and 7:19.

_____

_____

_____

Have you ever felt the way that the Apostle Paul felt? Explain.

_____

_____

_____

6. In Philippians 1:6, what hope does the Apostle Paul give us?

_____

_____

7. What weakness does Moses claim to have in Exodus 4:10?

_____

_____

8. What does Acts 7:22 state about Moses?

_____

_____

9. What weakness did Peter and John have in Acts 4:13?

_____

_____

How did this weakness not hinder them?

_____

_____

10. In 1 Timothy 5:23, what weakness does Timothy have?

_____

_____

11. Timothy appears to have had many weaknesses, but what does the Apostle Paul call him in 1 Timothy 6:11?

_____

_____

12. The Apostle Paul talks about weaknesses that can make us stronger. In your own words, summarize what he says in 2 Corinthians 12:7-10.

_____

_____

_____

_____

_____

13. List some of your strengths and weaknesses, the things that you do well and the areas of your life that need improvement.

_____

_____

_____

_____

_____

_____

_____

_____

_____

Chapter 4

Man And Men

In our modern society, guys want to be and often are considered men at an early age. It is an insult to call a young man "boy" or "son" and not refer to him as a "man." This is very different, however, from what we see in the Bible. In the book of Proverbs, the teacher continually addresses the student as "son." Likewise, the Apostle Paul uses the term "son" with Timothy. In both cases, they were most likely speaking to a young man, but the term "son" apparently did not offend them. Males were not fully regarded as men until they were around thirty years of age. Manhood was attained after one had grown in wisdom and understanding.

The principle of older men teaching younger men can be found throughout the Bible. Since older men had been through many joys and trials, they were seen as having a much fuller perspective on life. Older men, who have walked with God for many years, can impart much wisdom to a young man.

Sadly, in our society, most young men wrestle with the questions of manhood by themselves. Therefore, their ideas about what it is to be a man usually come from what they learn on their own. As a result, many men develop a distorted view of what it means to be a man.

In addition to a man's relationship with older men, another area of great importance is his relationship with his peers. A man needs to seek out companions in his age group that will have a positive impact on him. David and Jonathan provide us with a good example. The book of 1 Samuel records how these two men greatly encouraged and challenged each other by their friendship. The Bible contains many other examples that show us how men can strengthen one another.

Proverbs 27:17 tells us that as iron is used to sharpen iron in a similar way one man can sharpen another man. Every man can benefit from positive interaction with other men. A vital concern for men should be to have older men as well as younger men in their lives that will challenge them to become the men God intended them to be.

In order to better understand your relationship with other men, carefully study the following Bible verses and answer the questions.

1. What principles can be drawn from 1 Timothy 5:1 regarding our relationship with other men?

_____

_____

_____

2. Explain how the "fathers" and "young men" are contrasted in 1 John 2:13-14.

_____

_____

_____

_____

_____

3. What are the younger men instructed in 1 Peter 5:5?

_____

_____

4. Explain in your own words the counsel given to young men in Ecclesiastes 11:9-12:1.

_____

_____

_____

_____

_____

_____

5. What does Proverbs 3:31 and 24:1 say that our attitude should be toward evil men?

_____

_____

_____

_____

Are you doing any of the things these verses say not to do? Explain.

_____

_____

_____

_____

6. At what age does Jesus begin His ministry in Luke 3:23?

_____

7. Before Jesus began His ministry, what does Luke 2:46 and 2:52 tell us?

_____

_____

_____

_____

Is this significant? Explain.

_____

_____

_____

8. In Mark 8:27-28, what question does Jesus ask His disciples that shows He understood He had a relationship with other men?

_____

_____

_____

9. How did the following men identify themselves?

The servant, Genesis 24:34-35 _____

_____

David, 1 Samuel 17:58 _____

_____

The prophet, 1 Kings 13:18 _____

_____

Amos, Amos 7:14 _____

_____

_____

Simon Peter, Luke 5:8 _____

_____

Paul, Acts 21:39 and 23:6 _____

_____

_____

_____

_____

What do their answers show us?

_____

_____

_____

_____

How would you identify yourself?

_____

_____

_____

_____

10. Jesus chose twelve men to be His close disciples. Together, they shared many experiences and unique times of fellowship. State what they did in the following verses.

Mark 14:22-26 _____

_____

Luke 11:1-4 _____

_____

John 13:3-5 _____

_____

11. In Luke 9:46, what was a problem among the disciples?

_____

_____

Give an example of this problem among men today.

_____

_____

_____

_____

12. David and Jonathan were best friends. Their friendship is an example of how men can encourage each other. Explain the value that David puts on Jonathan's friendship in 2 Samuel 1:26.

_____

_____

_____

_____

13. List some older and younger men who have had a positive impact on your development as a man and explain how they have done so.

_____

_____

_____

_____

_____

_____

_____

14. List some older and younger men who are currently having an impact on your development as a man and explain how they are doing so.

_____

_____

_____

_____

_____

_____

_____

_____

Chapter 5

Man And Women

God has set forth in His word many principles regarding the way He intended men and women to interact. One of the most important Bible passages showing God's desire is 1 Timothy 5:1-2. In these verses, the Apostle Paul tells Timothy to treat the "elder women as mothers; the younger as sisters, with all purity." From these verses, we can see that a man's relationship to older women should be based on honor and respect, and that his relationship to younger women should be marked by purity of thought and actions. In both cases, he should have genuine love and concern for that individual as he would for a family member.

Although the proper relationship to older women is very important for a man to remember, probably the more difficult relationship for a man to keep in the right perspective is with the younger women. The idea of treating the younger women like sisters and with purity is normally far from most men's minds, yet this is the way God intended men to think in regard to the younger women. Just as a man is concerned about his own sister, he should be concerned in the same way about the welfare of other young women. Most young women would probably see this behavior as odd, but the godly woman will recognize this as the way that God intended men and women to behave.

God has laid down other guidelines in His word regarding the distinct roles of men and women. He has uniquely created each to fulfill specific purposes. Both men and women have very important roles, yet very different ones. Therefore, a void will exist if either one is not fulfilling their role.

The differing roles of men and women are part of God's plan to make men and women dependent on each other. The interdependence of men and women and our dependence on God is stressed in 1 Corinthians 11:11-12, "neither is the man without the woman, neither the woman without the man, in the Lord. For as the woman is of the man, even so is the man also by the woman; but all things of God." The God-fearing man and woman will realize the importance of each other's roles and study the word of God to know how these roles should be fulfilled.

The following questions deal with some important Bible verses regarding the roles and relations of men and women. By carefully examining these verses, a better understanding of God's desire for both men and women will be attained.

1. Read 1 Timothy 5:1-2. Give some practical examples of how men are to treat:

The older women

_____

_____

_____

_____

The younger women

_____

_____

_____

_____

_____

2. Read John 19:25-27. Why do you think Jesus said this?

_____

_____

_____

3. What word is used with the woman in Romans 16:1 that describes a family type of relationship?

_____

4. Read Proverbs 7:6-27.

How is this man described in verse 7?

_____

_____

_____

What is one of the main ways the woman seduces him in verse 21?

_____

_____

_____

How should verse 21 be a warning to us?

_____

_____

_____

Give some examples of how you might follow the counsel given in verses 24-25.

_____

_____

_____

5. How does 1 Corinthians 7:1-2 stress the idea of purity in relation to women?

_____

_____

_____

6. What quality in a woman is considered most important in Proverbs 31:30?

_____

_____

7. How are men and women different in 1 Corinthians 11:7-10?

_____

_____

_____

_____

_____

8. How are men and women the same in 1 Corinthians 11:11-12?

_____

_____

_____

_____

_____

9. Titus 2:3-5 describes an important ministry of the older women. What is it and why is it important?

_____

_____

_____

Is this ministry being done today? Explain.

_____

_____

_____

10. Does 1 Timothy 2:12 put responsibility on men?
Explain.

_____

_____

_____

_____

11. Do the roles and relationships of men and women
according to the Bible differ from society's view? Explain.

_____

_____

_____

_____

_____

_____

_____

Chapter 6

Man And Work

As we saw in Chapter 1 God And Man, one of Adam's responsibilities in the Garden of Eden was to work. Apparently, his work there was easy and enjoyable. However, after Adam sinned, God banished him from the garden and sent him out to work in the surrounding land. In addition, Genesis 3:17-19 tells us that God cursed the ground. The curse made the ground more difficult to cultivate. As a result, Adam had to work much harder to provide for himself and his family.

We can see clearly that both before Adam sinned and afterward, God gave him the responsibility to work. However, God greatly increased the burden on Adam after he had sinned.

The judgment that God placed on Adam can also be seen as a blessing. As a result of the curse, man would be much more challenged to provide for himself. He would have to overcome greater obstacles. Therefore, he would need to become more industrious and resourceful. He would be stretched and forced to grow as a man.

Work is something that challenges men. Through work, men become responsible and develop many important qualities that help them become the men that God intended them to be. Throughout the Bible, men have fulfilled their responsibility to work by a variety of occupations.

The following verses look at a man's responsibility to work and some of the occupations of men in the Bible. In addition, the verses deal with the attitude and motivation that a man should have in regard to work. Carefully study each Bible verse and answer the questions.

1. In Genesis 2:1-3, what did God do during the first six days of creation?

_____

_____

_____

2. Read Exodus 20:8-11. This command has two parts. We usually focus on what we are not to do, however, what does this command instruct us to do?

_____

_____

3. Explain the meaning of 1 Thessalonians 4:11-12 in your own words.

_____

_____ — _____

_____

_____

4. In 2 Thessalonians 3:10-12, a strict command is given in regard to anyone who will not work. When would this command apply and when would it not apply?

_____

_____

_____

_____

_____

_____

5. In Ecclesiastes 3:12-13, how is work described?

_____

_____

6. In Ecclesiastes 5:12, what benefit does the working man have?

_____

_____

7. In Nehemiah 4:6, what was the mindset of the people?

_____

_____

8. We can have the wrong motivation for working. What are some wrong motivations described in the following verses?

Ecclesiastes 4:4 _____

_____

Ecclesiastes 6:7 _____

_____

9. The following verses mention some of the occupations of men in the Bible. Write the occupations stated.

Genesis 4:2 _____

_____

Exodus 35:35 _____

_____

1 Chronicles 9:33 _____

1 Chronicles 22:15 _____

_____

Jonah 1:5 _____

Matthew 9:9 _____

Mark 1:16 _____

Acts 18:2-3 _____

Colossians 4:14 _____

Titus 3:13 _____

10. Compare Proverbs 10:4 and 22:29. What can be learned from these verses?

_____

_____

_____

_____

11. The main motivation we should have in doing our work is given in Colossians 3:23-24. Explain these verses in your own words.

_____

_____

_____

_____

_____

12. What is your motivation and attitude in regard to work?

_____

_____

_____

_____

_____

_____

_____

_____

_____

13. Are you fulfilling your responsibility as a man to work? Explain.

_____

_____

_____

_____

_____

_____

_____

_____

_____

Chapter 7

Man And Wisdom

Since the days of Adam and Eve, wisdom has been desired and sought after. Genesis 3:6 tells us that Eve desired the fruit of the tree of the knowledge of good and evil because she "saw the tree was good for food, and that it was pleasant to the eyes, and a tree to be desired to make one wise." Therefore, Eve took the fruit and ate it. She also gave the fruit to Adam and he ate it. Sadly, Adam and Eve listened to the lies of Satan rather than the wisdom of God.

Throughout the Bible, men are instructed to be wise. Countless men have come to ruin because of unwise decisions and conduct. One of the most important things for a man to possess is wisdom. In Proverbs 4:5-7, the teacher stresses to his student, "Get wisdom . . . Wisdom is the principal thing: therefore get wisdom."

Wisdom has truly long been a prized quality by men. People traveled great distances to hear the wisdom of King Solomon. Huge crowds followed Jesus to listen to the wisdom of His teaching, and a congregation in the Book of Acts selected Stephen and six others because they were full of wisdom.

Although it appears that God may give more wisdom to some men than others, He promises to give wisdom generously to all who call on Him. Wisdom is an essential quality in becoming the men God intended us to be. There is perhaps no greater reproach for a man than to be regarded as a fool. Therefore, let us hear the cries of scripture and be wise men.

The following verses look at some wise men and some foolish men in the Bible. In addition, the verses examine some of the commands in the Bible for us to be wise. Carefully consider each Bible verse and answer the questions.

1. Read Proverbs 8:32-36.

What instructions are given in verses 32-33?

_____

_____

_____

_____

_____

In verses 34-35, what are the results of obeying these instructions?

_____

_____

_____

_____

How does verse 36 portray someone who does not pursue wisdom?

_____

_____

_____

_____

2. Explain Proverbs 9:7-9 in your own words.

_____

_____

_____

_____

_____

_____

3. In Proverbs 26:12, what kind of man has little hope of being wise?

_____

_____

4. The men in the following verses all display some special kind of wisdom or ability. State the specific way they were wise.

The assistants of Moses, Exodus 18:25-26 _____

_____

Samuel, 1 Samuel 3:19 _____

_____

Men of Issachar, 1 Chronicles 12:32 _____

_____

The king's wise men, Esther 1:13-15 _____

_____

Daniel, Daniel 1:17 _____

_____

The wise men, Matthew 2:1-2 _____

_____

5. Joseph had great wisdom. How far did this wisdom take him in Genesis 41:39-46?

_____

_____

_____

_____

_____

_____

_____

6. The wise man and the fool are often contrasted in the Bible. In the correct column, write the differences between the wise man and the fool for each Bible verse.

Wise Man   **Fool**

_____   _____

_____   _____

Proverbs 3:35

_____   _____

_____   _____

Proverbs 10:1

_____   _____

_____   _____

Proverbs 10:14

_____   _____

_____   _____

Proverbs 12:15

_____   _____

_____   _____

Proverbs 13:20

Wise Man	**Fool**
_____	_____
_____	_____

Proverbs 14:16

_____   _____

_____   _____

Proverbs 15:2

_____   _____

_____   _____

Proverbs 29:11

_____   _____

_____   _____

Ecclesiastes 7:4

_____   _____

_____   _____

Ecclesiastes 10:2

_____   _____

_____   _____

Ecclesiastes 10:12

Briefly examine the columns for the wise man and for the fool. Write down any thoughts or observations you have.

_____

_____

_____

_____

_____

_____

_____

_____

7. Read Matthew 7:24-27.

Who does Jesus compare to the wise man?

_____

_____

_____

Who does Jesus compare to the foolish man?

_____

_____

_____

8. What are we instructed in Ephesians 5:15?

_____

_____

9. What is the Apostle Paul's rebuke to the Corinthian church in 1 Corinthians 6:5?

_____

_____

10. Mark 12:28-30 commands us to love the Lord in four different ways. Which one of these ways implies the idea of wisdom?

_____

_____

Give some examples of how you can apply this part of the commandment.

_____

_____

_____

_____

11. Name some other wise men or foolish men in the Bible.

_____

_____

_____

_____

_____

_____

12. The Bible has a strong emphasis for a man to be wise. In what areas of your life are you acting as a wise man? Explain.

_____

_____

_____

_____

_____

_____

_____

_____

_____

_____

13. In what areas of your life do you need to act wiser? Explain.

_____

_____

_____

_____

_____

_____

_____

_____

_____

Chapter 8

Man And Muscles

In Genesis 1:27, we read that God created man in His own image and that He created them "male and female." God has wonderfully designed and created the human body. Each body, both male and female, God has uniquely and beautifully sculpted. However, despite the marvel and beauty of the human body, most Christian men's books address only the spiritual aspects of being a man. Without question, the spiritual aspects are the most important, but the physical aspects cannot be disregarded.

A man's physical characteristics and condition have a bearing on how others view him as well as how he views himself. For example, people often regard men that have a deep voice or facial hair as being masculine.

Similarly, people are usually impressed by men who are strong or possess a muscular physique. The favorite Bible stories of many even include people such as Samson or Goliath.

Within the topic of the physical attributes of man, the subject of muscles and strength is probably the most controversial. One man who appears to have had the proper perspective on this subject was Jim Elliot, a missionary who was martyred in Ecuador. Jim Elliot desired to serve the Lord with all his strength. While attending Wheaton College, he was a wrestler. In a letter to his mother he wrote, "I wrestle solely for the strength and co-ordination of muscle tone that the body receives while working out, with the ultimate end that of presenting a more useful body as a living sacrifice." [5]

In another letter, Jim Elliot commented about wrestling saying:

> It's sure a good feeling not to be waterlogged and flabby while studying. I think it definitely stimulates the entire body process, including thinking, to be more physically alert. Like the horse in Job, one can rejoice in his strength. [6]

The following questions deal with man's physical characteristics and condition. Most of the questions have to do with the subject of muscles and strength. The word "strength" which is used in many of the Bible verses, most likely has a broader meaning of not only strength, but overall physical condition. To help you formulate a balanced, biblical view about the physical aspects of being a man, carefully read the Bible verses and answer the questions.

1. How does King David view the human body in Psalm 139:13-14?

_____

_____

_____

_____

_____

2. What differences can be seen between these two brothers in Genesis 25:23-27 and 27:11?

_____

_____

_____

_____

3. In Song of Solomon 5:10-16, the wife uses figurative language to impressively describe the appearance of her husband. Give your interpretation of his appearance.

_____

_____

_____

_____

_____

4. The family of Obed-edom was physically fit. How are they described in 1 Chronicles 26:8?

_____

_____

5. In 1 Chronicles 12:1-2 and 12:8, some of King David's "mighty men" are described. They obviously were gifted athletically, but probably also trained hard. What were some of their abilities?

_____

_____

_____

_____

6. In Zechariah 8:9 and 8:13, God gives an exhortation for the people to be strong in their work to rebuild the temple. What phrase does He repeat in both verses?

_____

_____

7. Explain Proverbs 20:29 in your own words.

_____

_____

_____

8. In Psalm 88:4, the psalmist describes his hopeless feelings saying that he has become like a man without what?

_____

_____

Does this sound serious? Explain.

_____

_____

_____

9. In Joshua 14:10-13, this older man was apparently in great shape. How does he describe himself?

_____

_____

10. In Psalm 18:32-34 and 18:39, King David talks about his strength. Is his attitude different from most men's attitude in regard to strength? Explain.

_____

_____

_____

_____

_____

11. Does 1 Timothy 4:8 teach against physical fitness? Explain.

_____

_____

_____

_____

_____

12. In Ecclesiastes 10:17, what subject does this verse address that relates to our physical condition and strength?

_____

_____

What is the attitude of the princes regarding this subject?

_____

_____

13. Explain your views on the physical attributes of man.

_____

_____

_____

_____

_____

_____

_____

_____

_____

Chapter 9

Man And Marriage

Marriage is a vital subject that all men need to understand. A single man must understand marriage for at least three reasons. First, the single man must prepare himself for marriage in the event that he marries. Second, a single man will interact with married couples so he needs to have an understanding of this important relationship. A situation may even arise where he will need to counsel a married couple. Third, the single man must understand marriage because the Bible often uses the marriage relationship as an illustration to help us understand other important subjects. For example, the Bible describes the relationship of Christ and the church as a marriage.

The married man has the added responsibility to understand the subject of marriage because he is actually in a marriage relationship. In 1 Peter 3:7, the Bible instructs husbands to live with their wife "according to knowledge." By learning about the marriage relationship, the married man will be able to better understand his wife and fulfill his role as a husband.

Although marriage is an important subject that men need to understand, most men invest little time trying to learn about marriage. Single men usually feel that they will learn about marriage when they marry. Married men usually feel that they are learning about marriage simply because they are married. Both views are incorrect. Before a man marries, he should begin learning about marriage. After a man marries, he needs to commit himself to understanding the marriage relationship. Even if a man never marries, he needs to understand this important relationship.

The following questions deal with some key concepts of marriage. Study each Bible verse carefully and answer the questions.

1. What marriage principles can be drawn from Genesis 2:22-25?

_____

_____

_____

_____

_____

_____

2. What command is given in Deuteronomy 24:5 concerning newlyweds?

_____

_____

_____

What principles can we draw from this command?

_____

_____

_____

_____

3. Based on Hebrews 13:4, how should marriage be viewed?

_____

_____

_____

_____

4. In 1 Corinthians 7:3-6, an important balance is stressed concerning the physical and spiritual. Why is this balance important?

_____

_____

_____

_____

_____

5. In 1 Corinthians 7:7-9, how does the Apostle Paul describe singleness?

_____

_____

_____

6. Read Ephesians 5:22-33. Explain how these verses put responsibilities on:

Women

_____

_____

_____

_____

_____

Men

_____

_____

_____

_____

_____

List some practical ways husbands could apply Ephesians 5:25-33.

_____

_____

_____

_____

7. In Isaiah 54:5-6, the Lord describes His relationship to His people. What words are used that pertain to marriage?

_____

_____

8. In 2 Corinthians 11:2, the Apostle Paul describes the relationship of Christ to believers. What words are used that pertain to marriage?

_____

_____

9. What principles can be applied to the relationship between a husband and wife based on God's relationship with His people?

_____

_____

_____

_____

_____

_____

_____

10. What instruction is given to fathers in Ephesians 6:4?

_____

_____

_____

List some practical ways fathers could apply the instruction of Ephesians 6:4.

_____

_____

_____

_____

_____

_____

11. Explain the impact a wife can have on her husband according to Proverbs 12:4.

_____

_____

_____

_____

_____

_____

12. Read Mark 12:18-25.

In verse 24, why were the Sadducees in error?

_____

_____

_____

In verse 25, what did the Sadducees not understand about marriage?

_____

_____

_____

13. Do you see any differences between the Bible's teaching on marriage and society's view of marriage? Explain.

_____

_____

_____

_____

_____

_____

_____

14. What are some ways you can learn more about the subject of marriage?

_____

_____

_____

_____

_____

_____

_____

_____

Chapter 10

Man And Spirituality

In the first and second chapter of Genesis, we see that God and man shared a beautiful relationship. This relationship, however, was broken when Adam and Eve sinned. Genesis 3:8 tells us that when Adam and Eve heard God walking in the garden they hid themselves from His presence. Genesis 3:9 shows God's deep desire for companionship with man as He calls out to Adam. In these verses, we see God seeking Adam, but Adam separated from God because of his sin. Throughout the centuries, we see the same, God desiring to have a relationship with men, but men separated from God because of their sin.

In 1 Corinthians 3:1-3, the Apostle Paul compares the Corinthian believers to men who have no relationship with God. He states that he could not speak to them as spiritual men, but as carnal men. The words of the Apostle Paul indicate that we are to be more than just men of flesh. God wants us to be more than just mere men. He wants us to be spiritual men. God desires that we be holy and that we have fellowship with Him. The prophet Micah declares that God requires man "to do justly, and to love mercy, and to walk humbly with thy God" (Micah 6:8).

Throughout the Bible, it is clear that for a man to be what God intended him to be, a man must have a personal relationship with God. The following questions look at God's desire for us to be spiritual men and some spiritual men in the Bible.

1. How is God's desire for a relationship with man expressed in Jeremiah 31:33-34?

_____

_____

_____

_____

_____

_____

2. Isaiah 43:6-7 mentions spiritual men and women who are God's sons and daughters and called by His name. What purpose do they fulfill?

_____

_____

_____

3. The Bible mentions many spiritual men. In the following verses, write the name of each man and how he is described.

Job 1:8 _____

_____

Matthew 1:19 _____

_____

Mark 6:20 _____

_____

Luke 2:25 _____

_____

Luke 23:50 _____

_____

2 Peter 2:7-8 _____

_____

4. Read Genesis 6:5-9.

What was man like in verse 5?

_____

_____

_____

What was God's feeling about man in verse 6?

_____

_____

_____

What does God intend to do in verse 7?

_____

_____

_____

What does verse 8 say about Noah?

_____

_____

How is Noah described in verse 9?

_____

_____

5. Based on Ecclesiastes 7:29, explain in your own words God's intention for man and how man has gone against it.

_____

_____

_____

_____

6. Read Psalm 119:9-11.

What answer is given to the question in verse 9?

_____

_____

_____

How is the young man obedient in verse 11?

_____

_____

_____

The question is asked in regards to "a young man." Do you think there is any special reason for this? Explain.

_____

_____

_____

_____

7. After considering the meaning of life, the author of Ecclesiastes reaches an important conclusion. Explain in your own words what he states in Ecclesiastes 12:13-14.

_____

_____

_____

_____

_____

_____

_____

8. Joshua was a spiritual man. In Joshua 1:6-9, what key words does God repeat to him?

_____

_____

_____

_____

How consistent was Joshua's meditation to be on the book of God's law?

_____

_____

9. King David and the Apostle Paul were spiritual men. Compare the command of King David in 1 Kings 2:2-3 to the command of the Apostle Paul in 1 Corinthians 16:13. How are the commands similar?

_____

_____

_____

_____

_____

_____

10. The commands of King David and the Apostle Paul are similar to the command that God gave to Joshua. How do all three of these commands emphasize that a man must have a relationship with God?

_____

_____

_____

_____

_____

_____

_____

11. How does the Bible's teaching on man and spirituality compare to society's view?

_____

_____

_____

_____

_____

_____

_____

12. If a man does not have a personal relationship with God, then he is not what God intended him to be. Do you have a personal relationship with God? Explain.

_____

_____

_____

_____

_____

_____

_____

If you would like more information on a personal relationship with God, please contact us. If you enjoyed this Bible study, please recommend it to your friends. Thank you very much.

Abidan

Publishers of Educational and Inspirational Books

www.abidanbooks.com

Bibliography

1. Smith, Ken G. *Learning To Be A Man*. Downers Grove, IL: Inter-Varsity Press, 1970, Back Cover

2. Halverson, Richard *Man To Man*. Los Angeles, CA: Cowman Publications, January 1961, p. 15

3. Spurgeon, Charles H. *The Saint And His Saviour: The Progress Of The Soul In The Knowledge Of Jesus*. New York, NY: Sheldon, Blakeman & Co., 1858, p. 193

4. Hillis, Don W. *Live With Yourself...And Like It*. Wheaton, IL: Victor Books, 1972, pp. 28-29

5. Elliot, Elisabeth *Through Gates Of Splendor*. Wheaton, IL: Living Books, Tyndale House, 1986, p. 16

6. Elliot, Elisabeth *Shadow Of The Almighty*. San Francisco, CA: Harper & Row, 1979, p. 42

Notes

CPSIA information can be obtained at www.ICGtesting.com
Printed in the USA
LVOW06s0136300114

371574LV00015B/232/P